HOUSEHOLD, LIFE,
EXPENSE TRACKER
& BUDGET LEDGER

Check out my hand drawn coloring books here

HOUSEHOLD, LIFE, EXPENSE TRACKER & BUDGET LEDGER

Help me buy more treats for my pets by reviewing this book here:

Undated Weekly Tracker with Monthly and Yearly Summaries for Structured Household Spending Across Medical, Pets, Personal Care, Subscriptions and Quality of Life

THIS YEAR BELONGS TO:

Start Date:

Year:

Contents

Contents	5
How this book works	7
Weekly Tracking Pages	11
Monthly Summary Pages	63
Subscriptions & Yearly Payments	67
Year End Total	69

HOW THIS BOOK WORKS

Modern life makes it surprisingly difficult to understand what we truly spend, because money leaves our accounts in many different ways:

- debit cards
- credit cards
- online shopping
- subscriptions
- automatic payments
- delivery apps
- in-store purchases

Because spending is spread across so many systems and accounts, I found I had no oversight of where my money was actually going or even how much I spent every month.
This book was created to gain back control.

The book does not offer a strict budgeting system, but a structured lifestyle expense tracker designed to help you understand:

- what you spend
- where you spend it
- and what your real cost of living looks like

The categories in this book are intentionally simple and condensed to keep the system practical and easy to maintain over time.

I do want you to remember that sometimes spending money on convenience, support, comfort, hobbies, dining out, delivery, or household help can protect your time, energy, health, or peace of mind.

This book is not designed to judge spending; its purpose is awareness.

Once you understand your real spending patterns, you can decide:

- whether your spending fits your budget
- where adjustments could help
- or where flexibility is reasonable and necessary

Everybody's life is different, you decide what is best for you.

This book is designed to work for:

- individuals
- couples
- families
- households with pets
- people with medical expenses
- and people with complex or changing lifestyles

Use this book as a flexible guideline, not a rigid system.

Writing things down by hand can also help create awareness in a way that typing often does not. There is a connection between our hands and our brain: the physical act of writing can make spending patterns easier to notice and remember over time.

Using a physical book instead of an app provides a mindful offline alternative that helps reduce screen time and doom scrolling

An easy way to use this book is to keep your receipts and fill in your entries when you return home. Online purchases can be written down immediately after pressing the "pay" button, while the purchase is still fresh in your mind.

This system is meant to support awareness, not perfection.

The categories in this book are designed to be flexible. You do not need to stress about perfectly separating every item on every receipt.
For example: if you went to a store mainly for household supplies and cleaning products, but also picked up a pair of socks or another small personal item, it is perfectly fine to record the entire receipt under Household & Supplies.

The goal is to understand general spending patterns over time, not to create complicated bookkeeping.

If you prefer more detailed tracking, another simple option is to separate purchases at checkout.

For example:

- household items on one receipt
- clothing or personal purchases on another

This can make tracking easier without requiring itemized calculations later at home.

Use the system in the way that works best for your household, energy level, and lifestyle.

Consistency is more important than perfection.

Weekly Total: ______

DATE / /

Groceries

Grocery trip 1: ______

Grocery trip 2: ______

Grocery trip 3: ______

Grocery trip 4: ______

Grocery trip 5: ______

Household & Supplies: ______

Online purchases: ______

Total: ______

Personal

Medical: ______

Personal Care (self): ______

Personal Care (professional): ______

Quality of life: ______

Transport: ______

Clothing: ______

Savings: ______

Total: ______

Pets

Total: ______

Notes

Weekly Total: ____________

DATE / /

Running Total: ____________

Groceries

Grocery trip 1: ____________

Grocery trip 2: ____________

Grocery trip 3: ____________

Grocery trip 4: ____________

Grocery trip 5: ____________

Household & Supplies: ____________

Online purchases: ____________

Total: ____________

Personal

Medical: ____________

Personal Care (self): ____________

Personal Care (professional): ____________

Quality of life: ____________

Transport: ____________

Clothing: ____________

Savings: ____________

Total: ____________

Pets

Total: ____________

Notes

Weekly Total: ____________

DATE / /

Running Total: ____________

Groceries

Grocery trip 1: ____________

Grocery trip 2: ____________

Grocery trip 3: ____________

Grocery trip 4: ____________

Grocery trip 5: ____________

Household & Supplies: ____________

Online purchases: ____________

Total: ____________

Personal

Medical: ____________

Personal Care (self): ____________

Personal Care (professional): ____________

Quality of life: ____________

Transport: ____________

Clothing: ____________

Savings: ____________

Total: ____________

Pets

Total: ____________

Notes

Weekly Total: ____________

DATE / /

Running Total: ____________

Groceries

Grocery trip 1: ____________

Grocery trip 2: ____________

Grocery trip 3: ____________

Grocery trip 4: ____________

Grocery trip 5: ____________

Household & Supplies: ____________

Online purchases: ____________

Total: ____________

Personal

Medical: ____________

Personal Care (self): ____________

Personal Care (professional): ____________

Quality of life: ____________

Transport: ____________

Clothing: ____________

Savings: ____________

Total: ____________

Pets

Total: ____________

Notes

Weekly Total: ______

DATE / /

Running Total: ______

Groceries

Grocery trip 1: ______

Grocery trip 2: ______

Grocery trip 3: ______

Grocery trip 4: ______

Grocery trip 5: ______

Household & Supplies: ______

Online purchases: ______

Total: ______

Personal

Medical: ______

Personal Care (self): ______

Personal Care (professional): ______

Quality of life: ______

Transport: ______

Clothing: ______

Savings: ______

Total: ______

Pets

Total: ______

Notes

Weekly Total:

DATE / /

Running Total:

Groceries

Grocery trip 1:

Grocery trip 2:

Grocery trip 3:

Grocery trip 4:

Grocery trip 5:

Household & Supplies:

Online purchases:

Total:

Personal

Medical:

Personal Care (self):

Personal Care (professional):

Quality of life:

Transport:

Clothing:

Savings:

Total:

Pets

Total:

Notes

Weekly Total:

DATE / /

Running Total:

Groceries

Grocery trip 1:

Grocery trip 2:

Grocery trip 3:

Grocery trip 4:

Grocery trip 5:

Household & Supplies:

Online purchases:

Total:

Personal

Medical:

Personal Care (self):

Personal Care (professional):

Quality of life:

Transport:

Clothing:

Savings:

Total:

Pets

Total:

Notes

Weekly Total: ____________

DATE / /

Running Total: ____________

Groceries

Grocery trip 1: ____________

Grocery trip 2: ____________

Grocery trip 3: ____________

Grocery trip 4: ____________

Grocery trip 5: ____________

Household & Supplies: ____________

Online purchases: ____________

Total: ____________

Personal

Medical: ____________

Personal Care (self): ____________

Personal Care (professional): ____________

Quality of life: ____________

Transport: ____________

Clothing: ____________

Savings: ____________

Total: ____________

Pets

Total: ____________

Notes

Weekly Total: ____________

DATE / /

Running Total: ____________

Groceries

Grocery trip 1: ____________

Grocery trip 2: ____________

Grocery trip 3: ____________

Grocery trip 4: ____________

Grocery trip 5: ____________

Household & Supplies: ____________

Online purchases: ____________

Total: ____________

Personal

Medical: ____________

Personal Care (self): ____________

Personal Care (professional): ____________

Quality of life: ____________

Transport: ____________

Clothing: ____________

Savings: ____________

Total: ____________

Pets

Total: ____________

Notes

Weekly Total: ______

DATE / /

Running Total: ______

Groceries

Grocery trip 1: ______

Grocery trip 2: ______

Grocery trip 3: ______

Grocery trip 4: ______

Grocery trip 5: ______

Household & Supplies: ______

Online purchases: ______

Total: ______

Personal

Medical: ______

Personal Care (self): ______

Personal Care (professional): ______

Quality of life: ______

Transport: ______

Clothing: ______

Savings: ______

Total: ______

Pets

Total: ______

Notes

Weekly Total: ____________

DATE / /

Running Total: ____________

Groceries

Grocery trip 1: ____________

Grocery trip 2: ____________

Grocery trip 3: ____________

Grocery trip 4: ____________

Grocery trip 5: ____________

Household & Supplies: ____________

Online purchases: ____________

Total: ____________

Personal

Medical: ____________

Personal Care (self): ____________

Personal Care (professional): ____________

Quality of life: ____________

Transport: ____________

Clothing: ____________

Savings: ____________

Total: ____________

Pets

Total: ____________

Notes

Weekly Total: ____________

DATE / /

Running Total: ____________

Groceries

Grocery trip 1: ____________

Grocery trip 2: ____________

Grocery trip 3: ____________

Grocery trip 4: ____________

Grocery trip 5: ____________

Household & Supplies: ____________

Online purchases: ____________

Total: ____________

Personal

Medical: ____________

Personal Care (self): ____________

Personal Care (professional): ____________

Quality of life: ____________

Transport: ____________

Clothing: ____________

Savings: ____________

Total: ____________

Pets

Total: ____________

Notes

Weekly Total: ________

DATE / /

Running Total: ________

Groceries

Grocery trip 1: ________

Grocery trip 2: ________

Grocery trip 3: ________

Grocery trip 4: ________

Grocery trip 5: ________

Household & Supplies: ________

Online purchases: ________

Total: ________

Personal

Medical: ________

Personal Care (self): ________

Personal Care (professional): ________

Quality of life: ________

Transport: ________

Clothing: ________

Savings: ________

Total: ________

Pets

Total: ________

Notes

Weekly Total: ____________

DATE / /

Running Total: ____________

Groceries

Grocery trip 1: ____________

Grocery trip 2: ____________

Grocery trip 3: ____________

Grocery trip 4: ____________

Grocery trip 5: ____________

Household & Supplies: ____________

Online purchases: ____________

Total: ____________

Personal

Medical: ____________

Personal Care (self): ____________

Personal Care (professional): ____________

Quality of life: ____________

Transport: ____________

Clothing: ____________

Savings: ____________

Total: ____________

Pets

Total: ____________

Notes

Weekly Total: ____

DATE / /

Running Total: ____

Groceries

Grocery trip 1: ____

Grocery trip 2: ____

Grocery trip 3: ____

Grocery trip 4: ____

Grocery trip 5: ____

Household & Supplies: ____

Online purchases: ____

Total: ____

Personal

Medical: ____

Personal Care (self): ____

Personal Care (professional): ____

Quality of life: ____

Transport: ____

Clothing: ____

Savings: ____

Total: ____

Pets

Total: ____

Notes

Weekly Total: __________

DATE / /

Running Total: __________

Groceries

Grocery trip 1: __________

Grocery trip 2: __________

Grocery trip 3: __________

Grocery trip 4: __________

Grocery trip 5: __________

Household & Supplies: __________

Online purchases: __________

Total: __________

Personal

Medical: __________

Personal Care (self): __________

Personal Care (professional): __________

Quality of life: __________

Transport: __________

Clothing: __________

Savings: __________

Total: __________

Pets

Total: __________

Notes

Weekly Total: ____________

DATE / /

Running Total: ____________

Groceries

Grocery trip 1: ____________

Grocery trip 2: ____________

Grocery trip 3: ____________

Grocery trip 4: ____________

Grocery trip 5: ____________

Household & Supplies: ____________

Online purchases: ____________

Total: ____________

Personal

Medical: ____________

Personal Care (self): ____________

Personal Care (professional): ____________

Quality of life: ____________

Transport: ____________

Clothing: ____________

Savings: ____________

Total: ____________

Pets

Total: ____________

Notes

Weekly Total: ______________

DATE / / Running Total: ______________

Groceries

Grocery trip 1: ______________

Grocery trip 2: ______________

Grocery trip 3: ______________

Grocery trip 4: ______________

Grocery trip 5: ______________

Household & Supplies: ______________

Online purchases: ______________

Total: ______________

Personal

Medical: ______________

Personal Care (self): ______________

Personal Care (professional): ______________

Quality of life: ______________

Transport: ______________

Clothing: ______________

Savings: ______________

Total: ______________

Pets

Total: ______________

Notes

Weekly Total: ______

DATE / /

Running Total: ______

Groceries

Grocery trip 1: ______

Grocery trip 2: ______

Grocery trip 3: ______

Grocery trip 4: ______

Grocery trip 5: ______

Household & Supplies: ______

Online purchases: ______

Total: ______

Personal

Medical: ______

Personal Care (self): ______

Personal Care (professional): ______

Quality of life: ______

Transport: ______

Clothing: ______

Savings: ______

Total: ______

Pets

Total: ______

Notes

Weekly Total: ______

DATE / /

Running Total: ______

Groceries

Grocery trip 1: ______

Grocery trip 2: ______

Grocery trip 3: ______

Grocery trip 4: ______

Grocery trip 5: ______

Household & Supplies: ______

Online purchases: ______

Total: ______

Personal

Medical: ______

Personal Care (self): ______

Personal Care (professional): ______

Quality of life: ______

Transport: ______

Clothing: ______

Savings: ______

Total: ______

Pets

Total: ______

Notes

Weekly Total: __________

DATE / /

Running Total: __________

Groceries

Grocery trip 1: __________

Grocery trip 2: __________

Grocery trip 3: __________

Grocery trip 4: __________

Grocery trip 5: __________

Household & Supplies: __________

Online purchases: __________

Total: __________

Personal

Medical: __________

Personal Care (self): __________

Personal Care (professional): __________

Quality of life: __________

Transport: __________

Clothing: __________

Savings: __________

Total: __________

Pets

Total: __________

Notes

Weekly Total: ______

DATE / /

Running Total: ______

Groceries

Grocery trip 1: ______

Grocery trip 2: ______

Grocery trip 3: ______

Grocery trip 4: ______

Grocery trip 5: ______

Household & Supplies: ______

Online purchases: ______

Total: ______

Personal

Medical: ______

Personal Care (self): ______

Personal Care (professional): ______

Quality of life: ______

Transport: ______

Clothing: ______

Savings: ______

Total: ______

Pets

Total: ______

Notes

Weekly Total: ______

DATE / /

Running Total: ______

Groceries

Grocery trip 1: ______

Grocery trip 2: ______

Grocery trip 3: ______

Grocery trip 4: ______

Grocery trip 5: ______

Household & Supplies: ______

Online purchases: ______

Total: ______

Personal

Medical: ______

Personal Care (self): ______

Personal Care (professional): ______

Quality of life: ______

Transport: ______

Clothing: ______

Savings: ______

Total: ______

Pets

Total: ______

Notes

Weekly Total: ____________

DATE / /

Running Total: ____________

Groceries

Grocery trip 1: ____________

Grocery trip 2: ____________

Grocery trip 3: ____________

Grocery trip 4: ____________

Grocery trip 5: ____________

Household & Supplies: ____________

Online purchases: ____________

Total: ____________

Personal

Medical: ____________

Personal Care (self): ____________

Personal Care (professional): ____________

Quality of life: ____________

Transport: ____________

Clothing: ____________

Savings: ____________

Total: ____________

Pets

Total: ____________

Notes

Weekly Total: ____________

DATE / / Running Total: ____________

Groceries

Grocery trip 1: ____________

Grocery trip 2: ____________

Grocery trip 3: ____________

Grocery trip 4: ____________

Grocery trip 5: ____________

Household & Supplies: ____________

Online purchases: ____________

Total: ____________

Personal

Medical: ____________

Personal Care (self): ____________

Personal Care (professional): ____________

Quality of life: ____________

Transport: ____________

Clothing: ____________

Savings: ____________

Total: ____________

Pets

Total: ____________

Notes

Weekly Total: ____________

DATE / /

Running Total: ____________

Groceries

Grocery trip 1: ____________

Grocery trip 2: ____________

Grocery trip 3: ____________

Grocery trip 4: ____________

Grocery trip 5: ____________

Household & Supplies: ____________

Online purchases: ____________

Total: ____________

Personal

Medical: ____________

Personal Care (self): ____________

Personal Care (professional): ____________

Quality of life: ____________

Transport: ____________

Clothing: ____________

Savings: ____________

Total: ____________

Pets

Total: ____________

Notes

Weekly Total: ____________

DATE / /

Running Total: ____________

Groceries

Grocery trip 1: ____________

Grocery trip 2: ____________

Grocery trip 3: ____________

Grocery trip 4: ____________

Grocery trip 5: ____________

Household & Supplies: ____________

Online purchases: ____________

Total: ____________

Personal

Medical: ____________

Personal Care (self): ____________

Personal Care (professional): ____________

Quality of life: ____________

Transport: ____________

Clothing: ____________

Savings: ____________

Total: ____________

Pets

Total: ____________

Notes

Weekly Total: __________

DATE / /

Running Total: __________

Groceries

Grocery trip 1: __________

Grocery trip 2: __________

Grocery trip 3: __________

Grocery trip 4: __________

Grocery trip 5: __________

Household & Supplies: __________

Online purchases: __________

Total: __________

Personal

Medical: __________

Personal Care (self): __________

Personal Care (professional): __________

Quality of life: __________

Transport: __________

Clothing: __________

Savings: __________

Total: __________

Pets

Total: __________

Notes

Weekly Total: ______

DATE / /

Running Total: ______

Groceries

Grocery trip 1: ______

Grocery trip 2: ______

Grocery trip 3: ______

Grocery trip 4: ______

Grocery trip 5: ______

Household & Supplies: ______

Online purchases: ______

Total: ______

Personal

Medical: ______

Personal Care (self): ______

Personal Care (professional): ______

Quality of life: ______

Transport: ______

Clothing: ______

Savings: ______

Total: ______

Pets

Total: ______

Notes

Weekly Total: ______________

DATE / /

Running Total: ______________

Groceries

Grocery trip 1: ______________

Grocery trip 2: ______________

Grocery trip 3: ______________

Grocery trip 4: ______________

Grocery trip 5: ______________

Household & Supplies: ______________

Online purchases: ______________

Total: ______________

Personal

Medical: ______________

Personal Care (self): ______________

Personal Care (professional): ______________

Quality of life: ______________

Transport: ______________

Clothing: ______________

Savings: ______________

Total: ______________

Pets

Total: ______________

Notes

Weekly Total: __________

DATE / /

Running Total: __________

Groceries

Grocery trip 1: __________

Grocery trip 2: __________

Grocery trip 3: __________

Grocery trip 4: __________

Grocery trip 5: __________

Household & Supplies: __________

Online purchases: __________

Total: __________

Personal

Medical: __________

Personal Care (self): __________

Personal Care (professional): __________

Quality of life: __________

Transport: __________

Clothing: __________

Savings: __________

Total: __________

Pets

Total: __________

Notes

Weekly Total: ____________

DATE / /

Running Total: ____________

Groceries

Grocery trip 1: ____________

Grocery trip 2: ____________

Grocery trip 3: ____________

Grocery trip 4: ____________

Grocery trip 5: ____________

Household & Supplies: ____________

Online purchases: ____________

Total: ____________

Personal

Medical: ____________

Personal Care (self): ____________

Personal Care (professional): ____________

Quality of life: ____________

Transport: ____________

Clothing: ____________

Savings: ____________

Total: ____________

Pets

Total: ____________

Notes

Weekly Total: ______

DATE / /

Running Total: ______

Groceries

Grocery trip 1: ______

Grocery trip 2: ______

Grocery trip 3: ______

Grocery trip 4: ______

Grocery trip 5: ______

Household & Supplies: ______

Online purchases: ______

Total: ______

Personal

Medical: ______

Personal Care (self): ______

Personal Care (professional): ______

Quality of life: ______

Transport: ______

Clothing: ______

Savings: ______

Total: ______

Pets

Total: ______

Notes

DATE / /

Weekly Total:

Running Total:

Groceries

Grocery trip 1:

Grocery trip 2:

Grocery trip 3:

Grocery trip 4:

Grocery trip 5:

Household & Supplies:

Online purchases:

Total:

Personal

Medical:

Personal Care (self):

Personal Care (professional):

Quality of life:

Transport:

Clothing:

Savings:

Total:

Pets

Total:

Notes

Weekly Total: ______

DATE / /

Running Total: ______

Groceries

Grocery trip 1: ______

Grocery trip 2: ______

Grocery trip 3: ______

Grocery trip 4: ______

Grocery trip 5: ______

Household & Supplies: ______

Online purchases: ______

Total: ______

Personal

Medical: ______

Personal Care (self): ______

Personal Care (professional): ______

Quality of life: ______

Transport: ______

Clothing: ______

Savings: ______

Total: ______

Pets

Total: ______

Notes

Weekly Total: ____________

DATE / /

Running Total: ____________

Groceries

Grocery trip 1: ____________

Grocery trip 2: ____________

Grocery trip 3: ____________

Grocery trip 4: ____________

Grocery trip 5: ____________

Household & Supplies: ____________

Online purchases: ____________

Total: ____________

Personal

Medical: ____________

Personal Care (self): ____________

Personal Care (professional): ____________

Quality of life: ____________

Transport: ____________

Clothing: ____________

Savings: ____________

Total: ____________

Pets

Total: ____________

Notes

Weekly Total: ____________

DATE / /

Running Total: ____________

Groceries

Grocery trip 1: ____________

Grocery trip 2: ____________

Grocery trip 3: ____________

Grocery trip 4: ____________

Grocery trip 5: ____________

Household & Supplies: ____________

Online purchases: ____________

Total: ____________

Personal

Medical: ____________

Personal Care (self): ____________

Personal Care (professional): ____________

Quality of life: ____________

Transport: ____________

Clothing: ____________

Savings: ____________

Total: ____________

Pets

Total: ____________

Notes

Weekly Total: ____________

DATE / /

Running Total: ____________

Groceries

Grocery trip 1: ____________

Grocery trip 2: ____________

Grocery trip 3: ____________

Grocery trip 4: ____________

Grocery trip 5: ____________

Household & Supplies: ____________

Online purchases: ____________

Total: ____________

Personal

Medical: ____________

Personal Care (self): ____________

Personal Care (professional): ____________

Quality of life: ____________

Transport: ____________

Clothing: ____________

Savings: ____________

Total: ____________

Pets

Total: ____________

Notes

Weekly Total: ______

DATE / /

Running Total: ______

Groceries

Grocery trip 1: ______

Grocery trip 2: ______

Grocery trip 3: ______

Grocery trip 4: ______

Grocery trip 5: ______

Household & Supplies: ______

Online purchases: ______

Total: ______

Personal

Medical: ______

Personal Care (self): ______

Personal Care (professional): ______

Quality of life: ______

Transport: ______

Clothing: ______

Savings: ______

Total: ______

Pets

Total: ______

Notes

DATE / /

Weekly Total: ____________

Running Total: ____________

Groceries

Grocery trip 1: ____________

Grocery trip 2: ____________

Grocery trip 3: ____________

Grocery trip 4: ____________

Grocery trip 5: ____________

Household & Supplies: ____________

Online purchases: ____________

Total: ____________

Personal

Medical: ____________

Personal Care (self): ____________

Personal Care (professional): ____________

Quality of life: ____________

Transport: ____________

Clothing: ____________

Savings: ____________

Total: ____________

Pets

Total: ____________

Notes

Weekly Total: ______

DATE / /

Running Total: ______

Groceries

Grocery trip 1: ______

Grocery trip 2: ______

Grocery trip 3: ______

Grocery trip 4: ______

Grocery trip 5: ______

Household & Supplies: ______

Online purchases: ______

Total: ______

Personal

Medical: ______

Personal Care (self): ______

Personal Care (professional): ______

Quality of life: ______

Transport: ______

Clothing: ______

Savings: ______

Total: ______

Pets

Total: ______

Notes

Weekly Total: ____________

DATE / /

Running Total: ____________

Groceries

Grocery trip 1: ____________

Grocery trip 2: ____________

Grocery trip 3: ____________

Grocery trip 4: ____________

Grocery trip 5: ____________

Household & Supplies: ____________

Online purchases: ____________

Total: ____________

Personal

Medical: ____________

Personal Care (self): ____________

Personal Care (professional): ____________

Quality of life: ____________

Transport: ____________

Clothing: ____________

Savings: ____________

Total: ____________

Pets

Total: ____________

Notes

Weekly Total: ________

DATE / /

Running Total: ________

Groceries

Grocery trip 1: ________

Grocery trip 2: ________

Grocery trip 3: ________

Grocery trip 4: ________

Grocery trip 5: ________

Household & Supplies: ________

Online purchases: ________

Total: ________

Personal

Medical: ________

Personal Care (self): ________

Personal Care (professional): ________

Quality of life: ________

Transport: ________

Clothing: ________

Savings: ________

Total: ________

Pets

Total: ________

Notes

Weekly Total: ____________

DATE / /

Running Total: ____________

Groceries

Grocery trip 1: ____________

Grocery trip 2: ____________

Grocery trip 3: ____________

Grocery trip 4: ____________

Grocery trip 5: ____________

Household & Supplies: ____________

Online purchases: ____________

Total: ____________

Personal

Medical: ____________

Personal Care (self): ____________

Personal Care (professional): ____________

Quality of life: ____________

Transport: ____________

Clothing: ____________

Savings: ____________

Total: ____________

Pets

Total: ____________

Notes

Weekly Total: ____________

DATE / /

Running Total: ____________

Groceries

Grocery trip 1: ____________

Grocery trip 2: ____________

Grocery trip 3: ____________

Grocery trip 4: ____________

Grocery trip 5: ____________

Household & Supplies: ____________

Online purchases: ____________

Total: ____________

Personal

Medical: ____________

Personal Care (self): ____________

Personal Care (professional): ____________

Quality of life: ____________

Transport: ____________

Clothing: ____________

Savings: ____________

Total: ____________

Pets

Total: ____________

Notes

Weekly Total: ____________

DATE / /

Running Total: ____________

Groceries

Grocery trip 1: ____________

Grocery trip 2: ____________

Grocery trip 3: ____________

Grocery trip 4: ____________

Grocery trip 5: ____________

Household & Supplies: ____________

Online purchases: ____________

Total: ____________

Personal

Medical: ____________

Personal Care (self): ____________

Personal Care (professional): ____________

Quality of life: ____________

Transport: ____________

Clothing: ____________

Savings: ____________

Total: ____________

Pets

Total: ____________

Notes

Weekly Total: ______

DATE / /

Running Total: ______

Groceries

Grocery trip 1: ______

Grocery trip 2: ______

Grocery trip 3: ______

Grocery trip 4: ______

Grocery trip 5: ______

Household & Supplies: ______

Online purchases: ______

Total: ______

Personal

Medical: ______

Personal Care (self): ______

Personal Care (professional): ______

Quality of life: ______

Transport: ______

Clothing: ______

Savings: ______

Total: ______

Pets

Total: ______

Notes

Weekly Total:

DATE / /

Running Total:

Groceries

Grocery trip 1:

Grocery trip 2:

Grocery trip 3:

Grocery trip 4:

Grocery trip 5:

Household & Supplies:

Online purchases:

Total:

Personal

Medical:

Personal Care (self):

Personal Care (professional):

Quality of life:

Transport:

Clothing:

Savings:

Total:

Pets

Total:

Notes

Weekly Total:

DATE / /

Running Total:

Groceries

Grocery trip 1:

Grocery trip 2:

Grocery trip 3:

Grocery trip 4:

Grocery trip 5:

Household & Supplies:

Online purchases:

Total:

Personal

Medical:

Personal Care (self):

Personal Care (professional):

Quality of life:

Transport:

Clothing:

Savings:

Total:

Pets

Total:

Notes

Weekly Total: ____________

DATE / /

Running Total: ____________

Groceries

Grocery trip 1: ____________

Grocery trip 2: ____________

Grocery trip 3: ____________

Grocery trip 4: ____________

Grocery trip 5: ____________

Household & Supplies: ____________

Online purchases: ____________

Total: ____________

Personal

Medical: ____________

Personal Care (self): ____________

Personal Care (professional): ____________

Quality of life: ____________

Transport: ____________

Clothing: ____________

Savings: ____________

Total: ____________

Pets

Total: ____________

Notes

Weekly Total: ______

DATE / /

Running Total: ______

Groceries

Grocery trip 1: ______

Grocery trip 2: ______

Grocery trip 3: ______

Grocery trip 4: ______

Grocery trip 5: ______

Household & Supplies: ______

Online purchases: ______

Total: ______

Personal

Medical: ______

Personal Care (self): ______

Personal Care (professional): ______

Quality of life: ______

Transport: ______

Clothing: ______

Savings: ______

Total: ______

Pets

Total: ______

Notes

Weekly Total: ____

DATE / /

Running Total: ____

Groceries

Grocery trip 1: ____

Grocery trip 2: ____

Grocery trip 3: ____

Grocery trip 4: ____

Grocery trip 5: ____

Household & Supplies: ____

Online purchases: ____

Total: ____

Personal

Medical: ____

Personal Care (self): ____

Personal Care (professional): ____

Quality of life: ____

Transport: ____

Clothing: ____

Savings: ____

Total: ____

Pets

Total: ____

Notes

Month:

Weekly Totals (Month Overview)

Week 1:

Week 2:

Week 3:

Week 4:

Total:

Monthly Fixed Expenses

Mortgage / Rent:

Phone:

Gas:

Water:

Electricity:

Internet:

Insurance:

Subscriptions:

Other costs:

Total:

Grand total:

Month:

Weekly Totals (Month Overview)

Week 1:

Week 2:

Week 3:

Week 4:

Total:

Monthly Fixed Expenses

Mortgage / Rent:

Phone:

Gas:

Water:

Electricity:

Internet:

Insurance:

Subscriptions:

Other costs:

Total:

Grand total:

Month:

Weekly Totals (Month Overview)

Week 1:

Week 2:

Week 3:

Week 4:

Total:

Monthly Fixed Expenses

Mortgage / Rent:

Phone:

Gas:

Water:

Electricity:

Internet:

Insurance:

Subscriptions:

Other costs:

Total:

Grand total:

Month:

Weekly Totals (Month Overview)

Week 1:

Week 2:

Week 3:

Week 4:

Total:

Monthly Fixed Expenses

Mortgage / Rent:

Phone:

Gas:

Water:

Electricity:

Internet:

Insurance:

Subscriptions:

Other costs:

Total:

Grand total:

Month:

Weekly Totals (Month Overview)

Week 1:

Week 2:

Week 3:

Week 4:

Total:

Monthly Fixed Expenses

Mortgage / Rent:

Phone:

Gas:

Water:

Electricity:

Internet:

Insurance:

Subscriptions:

Other costs:

Total:

Grand total:

Month:

Weekly Totals (Month Overview)

Week 1:

Week 2:

Week 3:

Week 4:

Total:

Monthly Fixed Expenses

Mortgage / Rent:

Phone:

Gas:

Water:

Electricity:

Internet:

Insurance:

Subscriptions:

Other costs:

Total:

Grand total:

Month:

Weekly Totals (Month Overview)

Week 1:

Week 2:

Week 3:

Week 4:

Total:

Monthly Fixed Expenses

Mortgage / Rent:

Phone:

Gas:

Water:

Electricity:

Internet:

Insurance:

Subscriptions:

Other costs:

Total:

Grand total:

Month:

Weekly Totals (Month Overview)

Week 1:

Week 2:

Week 3:

Week 4:

Total:

Monthly Fixed Expenses

Mortgage / Rent:

Phone:

Gas:

Water:

Electricity:

Internet:

Insurance:

Subscriptions:

Other costs:

Total:

Grand total:

Month:

Weekly Totals (Month Overview)

Week 1:

Week 2:

Week 3:

Week 4:

Total:

Monthly Fixed Expenses

Mortgage / Rent:

Phone:

Gas:

Water:

Electricity:

Internet:

Insurance:

Subscriptions:

Other costs:

Total:

Grand total:

Month:

Weekly Totals (Month Overview)

Week 1:

Week 2:

Week 3:

Week 4:

Total:

Monthly Fixed Expenses

Mortgage / Rent:

Phone:

Gas:

Water:

Electricity:

Internet:

Insurance:

Subscriptions:

Other costs:

Total:

Grand total:

Month:

Weekly Totals (Month Overview)

Week 1: ____________________

Week 2: ____________________

Week 3: ____________________

Week 4: ____________________

Total: ____________________

Monthly Fixed Expenses

Mortgage / Rent: ____________________

Phone: ____________________

Gas: ____________________

Water: ____________________

Electricity: ____________________

Internet: ____________________

Insurance: ____________________

Subscriptions: ____________________

Other costs: ____________________

____

____

____

Total: ____________________

Grand total: ____________________

Month:

Weekly Totals (Month Overview)

Week 1: ____________________

Week 2: ____________________

Week 3: ____________________

Week 4: ____________________

Total: ____________________

Monthly Fixed Expenses

Mortgage / Rent: ____________________

Phone: ____________________

Gas: ____________________

Water: ____________________

Electricity: ____________________

Internet: ____________________

Insurance: ____________________

Subscriptions: ____________________

Other costs: ____________________

____

____

____

Total: ____________________

Grand total: ____________________

Yearly Subscriptions

Total:

Yearly Payments

Total:

YEAR-END TOTAL

MONTHLY GRAND TOTALS

Month 1: ______________________

Month 2: ______________________

Month 3: ______________________

Month 4: ______________________

Month 5: ______________________

Month 6: ______________________

Month 7: ______________________

Month 8: ______________________

Month 9: ______________________

Month 10: ______________________

Month 11: ______________________

Month 12: ______________________

Once a year: ______________________

Once a year: ______________________

TOTAL
YEARLY
EXPENSES: ______________________

Aafke Art is a lifelong artist, painter and illustrator. She is also a blogger, translator and writer and published coloring books and illustrated classics. She tries to get some work done in-between walks with Antar; the Luxury Hound, visits to The Tarq; her deeply spoiled Horse, and frequent distractions by Paloma Pearl; the most beautiful Studio Pigeon in the world.

The text of the Household Life and Expense Tracker is printed in Glacial Indifference, designed by Hanken Design Co. Sans typefaces became popular in the early twentieth century. A Sans Typeface is easier to read for neurodivergent people. The titles are printed in Garamond. Claude Garamond (c. 1499-1561), a French punch-cutter and type designer active during the 16th century, was for a long time considered the primary designer of this typeface. However, many modern "Garamond" revivals are actually based on the work of Jannon, a French engraver whose 1615 designs were long misattributed to Garamond. The embellishments are mostly old engravings and illustrations originally printed in old books. This book was created and designed by Aafke Art, because she needs it for herself.

Made in the USA
Monee, IL
04 November 2026

67386644R00042